JUMPING S

SPIDERS DISCOVERY LIBRARY

Jason Cooper

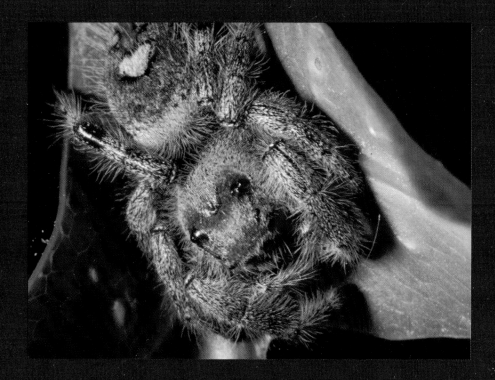

Rourke

Publishing LLC
Vero Beach, Florida 32964

ISBN-13: 978-0-8249-5142-9

www.rourkepublishing.com

PHOTO CREDITS: All photos © James H. Carmichael except title page © Lynn M. Stone

Title page: *A regal jumping spider waits and watches for prey.*

Editor: Frank Sloan

Cover and interior design by Nicola Stratford

Library of Congress Cataloging-in-Publication Data

Cooper, Jason, 1942-
  Jumping spiders / Jason Cooper.
     p. cm. -- (Spiders discovery)
  Includes index.
  1. Jumping spiders--Juvenile literature. I. Title.
  QL458.42.S24C66 2006
  595.4'4--dc22
                                    2005010729

Printed in Mexico

Table of Contents

Jumping Spiders

A jumping spider can jump perhaps 30 or 40 times its own length!

Jumping spiders get the punch in their jump from their fourth pair of legs. Jumping is this spider's way to escape danger and to find food.

Colorful jumping spiders are expert jumpers.

Most jumping spiders have 8 eyes. A few **species** have 10 and 12 eyes. Unlike many other kinds of spiders, jumping spiders see very well. Jumping spiders are amazing little creatures. Like all spiders, they are **arachnids**.

Spider scientists are known as **arachnologists**. They believe many jumping spiders can identify living objects 4 to 8 inches (10 to 20 centimeters) away. That means a jumping spider can tell another spider from **prey**.

Keen eyes help jumping spiders catch prey.

Arachnologists believe that jumping spiders can solve difficult problems in getting from one place to another. They also have shown an ability to learn from their mistakes.

A jumping spider retreats to its silken pouch.

Very few jumping spiders make large silk webs. But jumping spiders are silk makers. They rarely leave a perch without attaching themselves to a silk thread. Arachnologists call these safety threads "draglines."

With a dragline, a jumping spider can quickly return to a perch by climbing up the dragline. Jumping spiders also make silk retreats in which to rest and make their **egg sacs**.

Silk threads anchor a jumping spider to its perch.

Predator and Prey

Jumping spiders are **predators**, or hunters. Like other spiders, they catch and kill prey. Jumping spider prey is usually an insect, such as a beetle, fly, or cricket. Sometimes jumping spiders eat the flesh of dead animals, like vultures do.

A workman's jumping spider holds its prey, a dragonfly.

Several kinds
of jumping
spiders look
like ants. That
helps them
sneak into a
group of ants
and eat them.

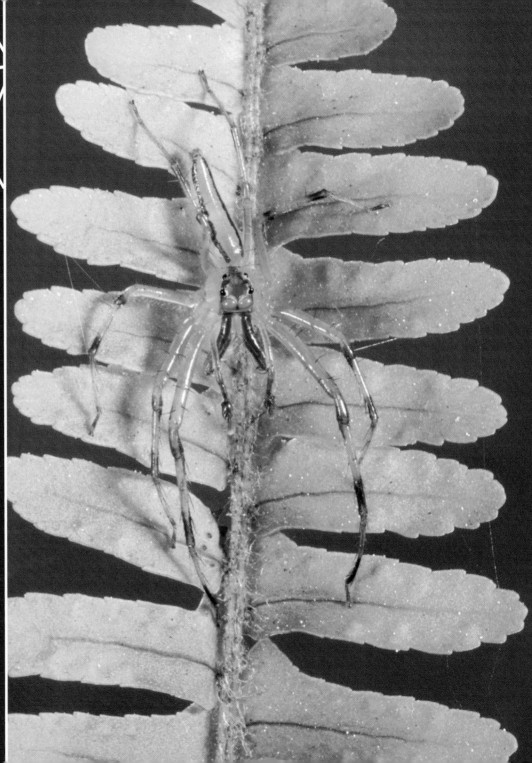

Some jumping spider species look much like their surroundings. This coloring helps keep them from becoming prey. Certain birds, wasps, and other predators eat spiders.

Jumping spiders hunt by waiting and watching. They may chase prey or creep cat-like after it. Then they jump onto prey and bite. Jumping spiders look for prey in many places. They can be found hunting on tree trunks, on buildings, and on the ground.

Jumping spider bites contain **venom**. The venom wouldn't hurt you, but it paralyzes or kills the spider's prey.

Ant or jumping spider? It has eight legs, so it's a spider.

A magnolia green jumping spider is a good color match for a Florida sword fern.

13

Where Jumping Spiders Live

There are probably 5,000 species or more of jumping spiders in the world. More than 300 species live in North America north of Mexico.

Most jumping spiders live in warm places. Look for jumping spiders in forests, fields, prairies, meadows, and outdoors around buildings. Certain kinds live in mountains.

This jumping spider lives in the warmth of Belize in Central America.

What Jumping Spiders Look Like

Jumping spiders are generally small. Most are hairy and much less than 1 inch (2.5 centimeters) in length. They are also colorful. The colors of some gleam in sunshine like metal. The colors come from both hairs and scales.

Jumping spider shapes are not alike, as the long Pike's slender jumping spider shows.

The red beauty jumping spider has bright colors and a hairy body typical of jumping spiders.

Like all spiders, a jumping spider has two major body parts—the **cephalothorax** and the **abdomen**. The eyes, head, mouth, and much of the stomach are in the cephalothorax. The abdomen is the plump part of the spider. It contains the silk glands, heart, lungs, and other organs.

Metallic colors and "headlight" eyes are typical of jumping spiders.

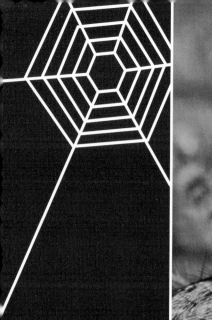

Jumping
spiders in the
United States
probably live
one or two
years. Females
probably live
longer than
males.

The Jumping Spider's Life Cycle

Jumping spiders lay eggs in a silk egg sac. Different kinds of jumping spiders lay eggs at different times.

In northern North America, many jumping spiders survive winter cold by **hibernating** in a silk sac.

Jumping spiders make silk egg sacs.

Jumping spiders help keep nature in balance by eating insects.

Jumping Spiders and People

Jumping spiders are small. They don't make big, lacy webs. Jumping spiders are easy to overlook.

Jumping spiders help keep nature's balance by feeding on insects and their eggs.

Glossary

abdomen (AB duh mun) — the second major part of a spider's body; the section that holds heart, lungs, silk glands, and other organs

arachnids (uh RAK nidz) — spiders and their kin; boneless, eight-legged animals with two major body parts and no antennas or wings

arachnologists (uh RAK nol uh jists) — scientists who study arachnids

cephalothorax (SEF uh luh THOR aks) — the body section of a spider that includes such organs as eyes, brain, venom glands, and sucking stomach

egg sacs (EGG SAKS) — cases or containers, usually ball-shaped, for eggs

hibernating (HI bur NAYT ing) — the act of spending cold months in an inactive state

predators (PRED uh turz) — animals that hunt other animals for food

prey (PRAY) — animals hunted and killed by other animals for food

species (SPEE sheez) — one kind of animal within a group of closely related animals, such as a *zebra* jumping spider

venom (VEN um) — a poison produced by certain animals, largely to kill or injure prey

Index

Further Reading

McGinty, Alice B. *Jumping Spider.* Rosen Publishing, 2003

Schwartz, David M. *Jumping Spider*. Gareth Stevens, 2001

Websites To Visit

www.americanarachnology.org/

www.uky.edu/Agriculture/CritterFileds/casefile/spiders/jumping/jumping.htm

http://everythingabout.net/articles/biology/animals/arthropods/arachnids/spiders/
   jumping_spider/

About The Author

Jason Cooper has written several children's books about a variety of topics for Rourke Publishing, including the recent series *Animals Growing Up* and *Fighting Forces*.